For you, beautiful Person?

Always the
best for you.

Paola Gauri

Nov, 2021.

Divine Intervention

The fine line between
life and death

Paola Garcia

Translated by Jocelyn Adele Gonzalez Junco

ISBN: 978-0-9992506-9-3
ISBN eBook: 978-0-9992506-8-6

The book *Divine Intervention—The fine line between
life and death* is entirely based on a personal
experience of the author. Its mere intention is to inform
the reader and contribute to the enrichment of his or
her search for emotional and spiritual growth, while
recognizing the values and believes of each and every
one of them.

Front cover image by Sebastian Matiz
Cover design: Mauricio Guerra

First published: July 2017.
Miami, Fl. USA.
Spanish version: *Intervención Divina—La delgada
línea entre la vida y la muerte.*

*Dedicated to those who need to find or uphold
that special light which is hope.
No matter the circumstances,
the last thing you may ever lose is faith.*

I am infinitely grateful to

My son Juan Sebastian, a wonderful gift who fills me with inspiration, pride, the will to live and to be a better person every day of my life.

David, a being of light who changed my life in a million ways from the first day we met. I always knew we had met for an extraordinary reason, but I could have never imagined that it would be that of literally "saving my life."

My parents: Pilar and Roberto. My siblings: Maria del Pilar, Jonathan, Ricardo, Martha, and my dear nephew Manuelito, for their unconditional love and support.

My doctors: Dr. Eric D. Hansen, Dr. Ricardo J. Komotar, Dr. Zoukaa B. Sargi, as well as their team of experts, assistants, and residents, for their eminence, merit, and knowledge.

And of course, Orquidea Ruiz, Andrea Vieira, and the extraordinary and passionate team of nurses, specialists, and administrators who are part of the Health System of the University of Miami, in particular, *Bascom Palmer Eye Institute* and *The University of Miami Hospital*, for their dedication to their work, their overwhelming kindness, commitment, and care. Thanks to all of you I was able to continue writing my story.

My ever-present aunts and uncles, cousins and friends all over the world, for being in my life; especially my cousin Carito. My friends Ross, Vanessa, Davide, and Marco, who have always and without hesitation given me their vote of confidence.

Finally, everyone who—whether deliberately or unknowingly—steered me towards the right place, at the right time.

Thank you!

Contents

In utter disbelief, eyes wide open, *Roland* asked:

"What did you hold on to? It must have been something very strong for you to be here today, as if nothing ever happened... so, tell me, what was it?"

"My faith. God." I replied, almost before she finished talking.

My name is Paola Garcia, but those whose hearts I have touched prefer to call me Pao, Paito or "la bonita."[1]

I was born on November 26th, 1979, and on April 26th, 2016, I was reborn... *intact.*

---

[1] Eng. "pretty face"

Week 1 – Psychedelia

Early March 2016. It has been almost four years since I came to Miami on June 26th, 2012, together with my son, Juan Sebastian, and practically against his will. He was sixteen at the time and was leaving behind, in Colombia, countless friends, cousins and everything that a boy at that age does not want to part from. And yet, here he was, with me: at the frontline—as always—a team, a family. A family of only two (mother and son), but a family nonetheless, together on the quest for opportunities for a better tomorrow. Him, somewhat reluctantly, ultimately wanting to go back, but still making an effort while we were here. Me, working up all my patience and creativity to make him change his mind.

On December 26th, 2015 we celebrated the end of the year by jumping out of a plane at fourteen thousand feet above land; something I always wanted, but never had the courage to do.

When you become mom and dad at fifteen you develop an almost "dull" sense of protection and safety that prevents you from taking risks. You become very aware that you must take care of yourself, not only for your own sake but for the sake of that new being who overflows you with love. At the same time, you develop dreadful fears that something bad might happen to him or her, so you look after yourself twice as much.

At any rate, Sebastian was already twenty years old and, almost without noticing, he went from being my son to being an accomplice and friend in every adventure. He persuaded me to join him with his adolescent scheme.

There I was, next to him, in a plane midflight in front of an open door, ready to jump. And I did! For a millisecond I felt that my heart hit my throat, I was not even able to scream, but just as fast that indescribable feeling of emptiness became a thrilling sensation of freedom. And so, there we were, mother and son, literally flying. Wow! A risky but fascinating experience that we are definitively going to remember forever, and the best part is that we experienced it together.

Among his new year's resolutions was an imminent return to Colombia, but somehow, for one reason or another, he did not accomplish it. He felt the need to wait a bit longer here in the United States, and I was, of course, happy.

We started the new year following our usual routine

When you move to a country such as the United States of America, you feel like time goes by faster. A month is barely started, and next thing you know, two months already went by. You begin your day with a long list of things to do, you think you will not possibly manage to take care of all of them, but somehow, as if by magic, you *do* find time for everything and you can even throw in a spontaneous undertaking that breaks the monotony of your day. And so, the days go by, vanishing right before your eyes... and you don't even notice it.

On a typically uninspiring day in the first week of March, I was in a meeting with Jorge, a member of the creative team at the company I had been working at for the past two years. We used to meet in a small living room in the second floor of the office. I was seated in a comfy sofa, laptop resting on my lap. Jorge was sitting in an unremarkable symmetrical chair, using a nearby table for his laptop, across the sofa, a bit to the left. We were laughing and coming up with new ideas, creating the messaging for a new ad campaign, when something happened. All of a sudden, I found myself frowning and squinting, eyes half closed; I couldn't quite understand what was happening, the scene before my eyes looked pixelated. I tried focusing my sight right above his head, on a white flat white wall behind him. I said:

–I'm seeing kind of weird.

–Weird? –he asked, looking at me.

–Yes, I don't know, I'm seeing something like little dots? Sort of… psychedelic!

He stared at me, not knowing what to say. We remained quiet for a moment, then I smiled, blinked my eyes slowly and we proceeded with the meeting without paying much attention to what had just happened.

It felt as if, for a moment, a filter with special effects appeared before my eyes, and just as suddenly, it disappeared. The event drifted quietly in my subconscious—*first warning sign*—, but it didn't amount to real concern at that point.

The mirror

I am one of those women who loves make-up, ever since I was a little girl. I remember my mother getting mad at me telling me over and over: "Don't put make up on! You're too young for make-up!" With time, I became a true expert—I can compete with professionals. I wear make-up almost every day, and depending on the occasion, I might put in the extra effort.

One afternoon towards the end of that same first week of March, as I was looking at the mirror while I was taking off my make-up, something in my eyes made me stare at them, because... I don't know how to explain it, but my pupils seemed different. There was an unfamiliar glow to them. It was not their color or *something* particular, they just seemed different. Lately, I was also starting to feel that my eyes were getting more tired than usual. —*Second warning sign*—.

Although, with time, I have become a very serene type of person, everything related to health quite alarms me. Much more so when it concerns the eyes, since I practically depend on them for work—they're my livelihood.

The first thing I thought was that perhaps my body was channeling the stress that way or I was overtired and my eyes needed a rest.

In a few days, my oldest brother Ricardo was coming to visit. It was a short trip, he was arriving the following Wednesday, so I took Thursday and Friday off to spend a bit of time with him. Thinking of those days ahead, I managed to relax. The thought of having him with me and the chance to take a break from the computer screen and the tense office environment encouraged me, even if it was only for a few days.

Week 2 – My father's vitamins

One week fuses into the next; I don't know what is happening to me; it is getting difficult to see small things—I had never had any issues with my eyesight. Each day that goes by my eyes feel more and more tired, I increase the size of the type in the PC screen and in my cellphone to avoid further straining my eyes; my colleagues at work are telling me that my eyes look red. I can't wait for my brother to come and finally take a long weekend off, far away from computers.

I need to relax… "everything is going to be fine."

WhatsApp: Wednesday, March 8th, 6:58 p.m.

"I'm in the parking lot of your building."

I'm so excited! Finally, the day arrives when my brother is home with me and Juan Sebastian. There is barely any time to do everything we want to do and have to do. But, first things first: dinner.

My brother Ricardo lives in Colombia with his wife Martha and little Manuel, so far my only nephew. He is the older of three siblings, five years older than me and ten years older than Maria del Pilar (Piti), my younger sister, who lives in Europe with her husband, Jonathan.

Ricardo is, for the most part, a reasonable and logical man; he has a strong personality and has always been a pillar of support and an example for the whole family.

While Sebastian, my brother and I were catching up on everything during our dinner, and without making a big deal out of it, I began telling him about my recent vision problems. He asked me casually:

"Do you have health insurance?"

"Yes, I do, through my employer."

"Maybe it's time for you to wear glasses, get an appointment with an ophthalmologist."

"Hmmm yes... Though, I think it's probably stress and exhaustion, I guess it's best to see a specialist," I said quietly.

Given my reply and the tone of my voice, I think he felt that I was somewhat unwilling to wear glasses, since I had never needed them before, so he started going through a litany of every family member who wore glasses, and even the reasons why they wore them: some of them because they were near-sighted, others far-sighted, while others for reading, etc. I looked at him and nodded in agreement, lowering my eyes.

When I was in college, pursuing the exciting career I chose to devote myself to—Marketing and Advertising—, *Cirque du Soleil* was one of the success cases we analyzed repeatedly. Ever since I saw them in video for the first time, I fell in love with their shows. I will never forget that feeling of longing and defiance that I felt watching them, thinking to myself no matter where or when, one day I am going to see them live.

In those days, the idea of leaving Colombia was nowhere near my thoughts, but you never know where life will take you, and a decade later in Miami, my son surprised me with tickets for one of *Cirque du Soleil*'s most magical performances— *Toruk*—inspired by one of the highest-grossing science fiction movies of all times: Avatar. Once again, my son was making my dreams come true.

The V.I.P. seat

"And now, what should we do with my brother?"

Sebastian had purchased the tickets almost a month in advance, when we didn't know Ricardo was coming, so what could we do? Buy an additional ticket. But now we had a problem—for that performance, there were only a couple of spots available—meaning, one of us would have to sit by him or herself. At any rate, that was not a setback for us and we went ahead and bought it. On the day of the show, I was the lucky one who took the solo seat. As it turned out, we had purchased a spot right in front of the stage and Sebastian and Ricardo decided I should be the one taking it, since I was having trouble seeing.

It was the first time that any of us was experiencing a Cirque du Soleil performance. I was ecstatic. For a couple of hours, immersed in the pure magic of the show, enveloped by the interplay of light and sound, transported to a parallel world of wonder, the impending distress caused by my eyes all but dissipated from my mind. It was a breathtaking experience.

The next day, one of our to-do's was to buy vitamins for our father; a mandatory stop in front of a huge rack of vitamins of all kinds and sizes.

There we were, the three of us, trying to fulfill my father's request. After scanning each and every shelf a couple of times, I sighed and told them:

"I am unable to see anything."

"You can't find them?" my brother asked.

"No, it's not that I can't find them. I cannot see ANYTHING AT ALL! I cannot read the names on the tags."

"Are you serious?" he doubted, holding the biggest container he could find, with the largest print possible. "Can you read that?"

…And I was unable to see anything!

—Third warning sign—.

On Friday, March 11th, my brother went back to Colombia and that very same day I set up an appointment for the first available date to see an ophthalmologist, which was March 21st, *in ten days*. Although it was not a date in the immediate future, I was feeling optimistic—I was finally taking charge of the situation. I chose the specialist with the most experience.

Week 3 – An unfamiliar world

The four days I took time off computers went by. According to my own *naive* analysis, my eyes were supposed to have rested and my vision improved, alas that was not the case.

I started blaming my age, with a pinch of sarcasm—well, let's face it, time is unforgiving, why would I be spared? It is my turn to start needing glasses—this is what I thought to myself and I occasionally shared with trustworthy co-workers at the office. I had, of course, told my parents about my symptoms, but didn't give them all the details. Whenever I called them, they asked whether there were any developments in that subject.

I remember that my mother, just as my brother, was also convinced that my problem would be solved with prescription glasses. She tried encouraging me by talking about how beautiful the frames were nowadays. She thought glasses were going to look great on me. She mostly blamed the computer, telling me I spent too much time in front of the screen and that I should rest my eyes more often. Lately, all of those phrases had become unavoidable, signature slogans emerging in every single call. *Oh mothers...*

Whether far or near, all things started getting blurry. I could not make out signs that only a few days before were perfectly clear with a mere glance.

With my face a couple of inches away from the monitor and huge type, work started to become an eight-hours-a-day torture. I was trying to avoid "public awareness" about the issue; I didn't want to breed uncertainty at work—who could ever imagine that the *only* copywriter in the whole company (at the time) was going blind? No! No way, I could not risk my job in the least.

A scream

At the workplace, and in general, I'm a very reserved person when it comes to my private life—personal problems or matters that affect me—but it was unavoidable, my colleagues would eventually notice that something was wrong. The font size in my computer was an unforgiving give-away.

The office is set up as an open space, so whomever would come near me could plainly see that something was definitively off with me.

Additionally, and because of my circumstances, I was starting to take longer than usual to meet requests, and when my coworkers opened the files I sent them, it was like *a scream* coming from their monitors, because I didn't realize I should have changed the *font* size that I was working with before saving and sending off. So, they were receiving and opening files with huge fonts.

It was Cecile, who sat to my left, the one who, upon receiving a text for an email message I created told me with a degree of unease "Hey *flaca*,[2] you're sending your files with huge fonts, is everything alright with you?"

A few minutes later, Mike—at the time, my boss, today, a friend— with a typical male "direct" approach, also asked me why I was saving files in enormous zoomed-in proportions.

The only thing I told Cecile was that my eyes were tired and I did not want to strain them, but that

---

[2] Eng. "skinny girl"

I had an upcoming appointment to see a specialist. I gave Mike additional details, but I could not share with him the extent of my problem.

They both gathered that indeed something was the matter, but I was going to solve it, so nobody made an issue out of it… *for the time being.*

The world of vision care, beyond the obvious basic care, had been unknown to me until then. If I remember correctly, I had only had two simple eye exams in my whole life, and in both cases I only recall the doctors complimenting my excellent eyesight.

Since I never had to do it, those two spontaneous past exams had been my only reference, but years go by, things change, and there I was, in front of innumerable webpages trying to find eyewear that I could fall in love with, looking for the perfect style that would fit my features and personality.

The truth is, I did not dislike the idea of wearing glasses, and if I had to, I had to! Period! In hindsight, I think I was psychologically preparing myself for the whole thing.

I usually adjust quickly to changes and this situation was not going to be the exception. So, I was going to make it the least traumatic possible. If I had to wear glasses from now on, I was going to find the ones that would captivate me each time I had to wear them. In other words, forever! By now, as far as the unmistakable problem with my eyes, I was convinced that the only time when I was going to do without glasses would be while I was sleeping. I had not yet seen a doctor, but I took it for granted that I wasn't going to get away with not wearing glasses and that was going to solve my problem.

Week 4 – A matter of logic

Another week began, the fourth one. My eyesight was going from bad to worse and as new warning signs were triggered, my anguish increased.

Burdened by the whole thing, but at the same time appeased, knowing I would solve the issue in a few days, there was something that did not fit into my logic. Although I don't usually arrive at conclusions when I do not know enough about the issue at hand, logic was telling me that such a radical deterioration in *such short time* was not exactly normal: "What is going on with my eyes? I only hope that it is not serious." I take a deep breath and tell myself: "Everything is going to be fine!" Six words that always manage to appease the chaos in my mind, as if by magic.

Nick and Jen (Chicuelitos,[3] as I affectionately call them), started working with me at the company on October 2014, almost on the same day I started. We were all hired by Mike to be part of his team— the Marketing team.

Since then, we have been very close. We had perfect synergy when it came to team work. We developed a lasting friendship, trust and support for each other. Working with them made my days fun and enjoyable. They were the only ones in the office I felt comfortable talking to and making jokes about my eyesight. Plus, both of them wore

---

[3] Eng. "little kids"

glasses, so I could ask them anything I could think of—and I generally do not think up very ordinary questions.

Black and White

That Monday afternoon, Nick showed me the final design of a digital banner we had been working on with Camila (one of the company's talented designers), which was ready to be uploaded to our blog.

"Have a look at how the banner turned out, do you like it?"

"Hmmm yes, but why didn't Cami color-in the model and instead left him in black and white? I think that makes it look flat, don't you?"

"Pao, that is not black and white! It's full color!"

He stared at me for a moment, in utter silence, and then broke it—as he usually does—bursting out a laugh, concluding: "Yep, you need eyeglasses!"

Although at the time he made a joke about it, I could see it in his face: there was an element of worry, the same subtle apprehension I had perceived in Cecile's and Mike's voices a few days earlier. I took in his words with a smile, conveying surprise and told him my appointment was coming up in two days. But the truth is that I had perfectly read in his face this was no small matter. Someone else's eyes had uncovered a new piece of the puzzle that I was unaware of: "color perception."

March 21st.

Never had I felt so excited to go to a doctor's appointment. I was relieved and convinced that this doctor with several decades of experience was going to fix my problem.

After a couple of routine tests with devices that were *totally new* for me, the real eye exam began. That's the one that we all know, where you have to read letters or numbers at the other end of the room: first with one eye, then the other, and depending on your ability, the doctor adjusts the lenses until they find the right combination that allows the patient to see clearly.

I remember the practitioner exhausted every possible combination that the instrument allowed; nothing helped me see clearly. He proceeded to open a shabby doctor's bag with hundreds and hundreds of lenses, and he started trying them out manually on me. I don't know if it was intuition or experience, but he ultimately arrived at a formula that he wrote down. I ordered my glasses based on that prescription at the same location, since they also had a shop selling all kinds of frames. I fell in love with a *Prada* frame, I think it was one of the most expensive ones there, but it didn't matter to me at the time. Remember what I said about the need to be captivated by the glasses I was going to choose? Well, this one was it! It had personality, and it was 100% Paola. If I was going to have to wear glasses from now on—for 17 hours a day, seven days a week—captivation was the least I could feel for these glasses. There was nothing else for me to do, but wait.

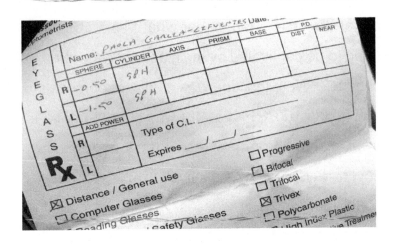

Week 5 – Disappointment

The sun becomes brighter, the intensity of lamps increases, they become huge reflectors that blind me. Words begin to fade on the computer screen, on my cellphone, on TV; I start having to ask Sebastian to help me read credit card numbers, my mail, etc. I literally begin to need "assistance!"

In the lapse of a month, my whole life was falling apart. This issue was demanding my undivided attention, like a snowball rolling down a hill, it was growing and becoming impossible to ignore. Solving the problem was beyond my control. I felt powerless! I couldn't wait to wear my glasses, I needed to regain my eyesight! I needed to get my life back!

March 28th.

Finally, the much awaited call comes:

"Ms. Paola, we are calling from the optician's office, your glasses are ready and you can come pick them up."

I went straight to the optical shop, without detours or diversions; it was close to my office so it took me about 15 minutes to get there.

Holding the glasses in my hands, I couldn't contain my excitement: "They are just divine! Thank you!" I exclaimed as I put them on... And then, the excitement vanished. The improvement was minimal! As I looked at my reflection in a mirror, I thought to myself "Maybe I have to get used to them, maybe it's normal, the eyes need to adjust.

Back in Colombia, my mother and brother were awaiting this moment with as much excitement as I, so I took a selfie and sent it to them. I called them later and they told me how great I looked wearing the glasses. I said "I might look good, but can't see much." Each of them, separately, but as if on cue, insisted that I had to wait a few days and get used to the new eyeglasses, and if they still didn't work for me, then I had to go back to the doctor's and tell him that the prescription was wrong or the lenses were not done properly... What joy to look forward to!

On my way back to the office and over the two days that followed, I started coming up with visual exercises with the new glasses: I put them on, took them off, blocked one eye, then the other and— surprise!—I saw much worse with my left eye. A few days prior, that was not the case.

Exasperation

March 30th.

Without an appointment and without previously calling to check whether the doctor could see me, I show up at the optician's office where I was tested and got my glasses. I tell them I do not know if it is due to the lenses or the prescription, but the glasses are useless to me.

The doctor who had tested me was not in at the time, instead, a much younger doctor heard my objection and offered to provide a second exam to determine what was wrong. I thought it was a good idea to have someone else do the test, someone younger. My initial theory about choosing an older doctor with "decades" of experience proved to be unfounded. By that time, I had already lost confidence in the first doctor. So, I willingly put myself in the hands of the new physician.

We started out the same way: first, the two devices that I was *by now* familiar with. Then, she begun the exam we all know—and again, went through an endless combination of lenses with hopeless results. The doctor asked me, "What letter do you see here?" I could only see a black, large smudge; an absolutely blurred image...

"Hm, I don't know... I can't see it."

"Make an effort!" she said, loudly and with a certain attitude.

I think the doctor was annoyed. For a moment, I thought she did not really believe I was unable to see any letters at all... maybe she thought I was lying? She repeated even louder, "What letter is this?!"

...For the first time since all of this had started, I burst out crying, enveloped by anguish and an indescribable sense of frustration. The doctor stepped aside, turned on the lights and asked surprised:

"What is the matter?"

"I really am unable to see anything. This has never happened to me before and every day that goes by it gets worse." I replied, trying to hide my face, my fingertips touching my eyebrows, overtaken with sorrow.

...She gave me a tissue to dry my tears and waited a few minutes until I got a hold of myself, before continuing the test. Her strong voice transformed into a troubled one, too; she halted the exam and started looking at my eyes through other devices.

When she concluded a series of tests that lasted over two and a half hours, she told me that she had to be honest with me. She said she did not see a distinct damage in my eyes, so we needed a third opinion. She was unable to reach a diagnose.

The doctor wrote down her concluding comments and the results of every exam, gave her report to me and asked me to show it to an ophthalmologist as soon as possible... Wait a minute, an ophthalmologist? So, she wasn't an ophthalmologist herself and neither was the doctor who had seen me previously? This is the part where I learned that opticians and ophthalmologists are not one and the same. I was without a doubt an ignorant fool in a world that I was only starting to get acquainted with — *and how!*

She also recommended I should get blood tests. This was key in order to determine the root of the problem: what was causing the "accelerated and inexplicable" loss of vision? Finding the underlying cause became a race against time.

The American health system has some similarities to that of other countries: depending on your healthcare plan, you might first need to see a primary care physician (PCP) before you can see a specialist; your primary doctor will get a referral for you, conditional to your illness or symptoms. This is synonymous with "time," something I had to leverage as much as possible. On the other hand, without the referral, I would have to go directly to a specialist and be fully responsible for the fees. It's not a secret that the quality of healthcare in the United States is high, however, the same goes for its cost, especially when you have to pay it out-of-pocket.

When I got home, with the report of my second exam in my hands, I immediately set out to get the first available appointment with a PCP, which was only at the beginning of the following week.

I thought it was a good idea to create a folder, documenting the results and files I got from my first and second visits to the opticians', the bill for the useless and *divine* eyewear, and the notes I was taking regarding dates, addresses, and names of new doctors. Something told me then that this was merely the beginning of a very necessary and lengthy chronological record that laid out a new medical history about my sudden an unexplained loss of vision.

Week 6 –The perpetual protocol

A new day begins and—with my typical positive outlook—I get ready for my doctor's appointment. I am full of faith and convinced that very soon, everything is going to be fine.

"Mom, do you want me to come with you?" Sebastian asks.

"No Loki, don't worry, you don't have to." I reply thankful, with a smile, placing my hand on his head.

The truth is, I preferred running these errands alone; I did not want to worry him too much.

My son is an extremely calm and reserved individual. In fact, very few things worry or distress him, but I know he pays special attention to everything that happens to me, and I really did not want to disturb his peace—his or anybody's! That's why I barely shared with anyone the intensity of the symptoms of decline that I was developing every day, with the exception of my optometrists.   And today, I was going to reveal these symptoms to a primary doctor, since my main objective was to get a referral to an ophthalmologist as soon as possible, and without any snags.

There I was, in a waiting room full of people, waiting for my turn to be seen by the *only* doctor in that office. I think there must have been ten people in front of me.   You can forget that your appointment is at this or that time! What good was that for?—At any rate, I did not want anything to derail the achievement of my goals, much less instigate bad faith in the doctor's office staff, so I patiently waited, in silence and ungrudging.

I finally heard my name, it was called up along someone else's. We went into another room, divided by a simple curtain. They took my blood pressure, asked a few questions and back I went into the waiting room.

After another almost 40 minutes, they called me again into the doctor's office, for an exchange that did not even last 10 minutes. The doctor asked me a few other questions about my medical history and was eager to get it over with, almost guessing my answers and jotting them down quickly: *Do you drink alcohol? Do you smoke? Are you allergic to any medications?* And so on. His only medical procedure was to place the stethoscope over my chest to listen to my heartbeat, after which he immediately sent me to *the room next door*, so that his assistants could then: do a full electrocardiogram, abdominal exam, neck palpation, as per the report, they even examined my head, though I actually cannot remember having had anything done related to the head, but anyway... I underwent a series of exams which were not the reason for my visit, but apparently every patient who went into that office had no choice but to endure.

I thought, "OK, since we're already here, let's do every possible test that he is requesting, let's rule out all possibilities. What if what's wrong with me has something to do with these tests?" So, I endured every exam, but not without reminding them that my priority was getting *my eyes* checked; I had to see a specialist for that and the objective of my visit was just to obtain that specific referral. Additionally, in the long list of exams they had to include a blood test requested by the optician in the report I brought with me.

When I showed it to the doctor, he read a few lines in the paperwork I gave him and agreed, "Yes, it says here you need to see an ophthalmologist." I merely sighed, but in my head there was a voiceless cry "Oh my God!" I looked at him in my best effort to fake a smile while he filled out the referral (I can't even begin to describe how sloppy this consultation was). "Well, he's already on the referral! This is what I needed to get, along with the blood tests," it was the one thing I was focusing on at the time.

Actually, all I wanted to do was run out of that place, but I couldn't. I had to "proceed to the little room next door."

Once they took the blood samples, completed the electrocardiogram, the abdominal exam, the neck exam, etc., I had to go into a waiting room where someone else explained to me that they would take care of making an appointment for me (for the Doctor's referral) with the pertinent ophthalmologist covered by my health insurance, and that they would let me know the date as soon as they had set up the appointment.

"Don't you worry Paola, the person in charge of setting up the appointments is very efficient. That's basically what she does all day long, so she knows who to speak to. When do you need the appointment for?" he asked.

I looked at him somewhat skeptical but, moreover, dreading that getting the appointment might take longer than usual. The fact was that the only person who was intent on procuring that appointment was me, and I was also the one who was afflicted by any delays in doing so.

This was the first time I was using my health insurance to see a specialist. Naively, I understood that the usual procedure for requesting a referral and getting a specialist appointment was in fact what the office staff told me, and I had no other choice but to put my faith on them.

"Great! If she can get the appointment for me as soon as possible, I will be very grateful. I am having some serious issues with my eyesight, so it is urgent to get the appointment," I said, smiling, trying to win them over.

"Sure, she will call you and will give you all the information once she sets up the appointment. Now, Paola, I'm going to give you a different appointment to come back and review your blood test results with the doctor."

Incompetence

It might have been intuition: my fear turned out to be true. The day came when I had to get the test results, but I never got the phone call with the appointment for the ophthalmologist, so that was the first thing I asked about when I came in. Of course, they replied with a series of excuses and as if they were absolutely on it. Once again, they promised to "insist" calling in order to get me an appointment and call me back at once as soon as they had it.

Needless to say, I was not very happy, but I couldn't show it. I said it was very important to obtain the appointment and I was depending on them—yet again—to set it up.

In contrast, the blood results were perfect. No abnormalities showed up; there was nothing to worry about. All other exams performed yielded the same results: perfect! On the one hand I was happy, according to these results I was doing great, so, any bad news was ruled out. On the other hand, and like a huge wave swallowing me, I was occupied with one thought, "Dear God, what is wrong with me, then?!"

Back to basics: the ophthalmologist, I'm sure that's where the answer lies; and what is more, the solution!

It is Friday, the end of the week and I do not hear back from the PCP's office regarding my appointment. I call them, they tell me the staff member responsible for setting up the appointments is sick and nobody else can do her job; she would be back on Monday...—*This can't be happening!*—My level of frustration and anger was massive. I knew it, I could not entrust someone else to understand how urgent it was for me to get that appointment.

Unfortunately, there was nothing else I could do until Monday.

Week 7 – Outlines

When I moved to America, I brought with me an extensive professional track record that began when I was 17-years-old, not only working for a series of large corporations, but also as an entrepreneur.

While I was in my senior year at college, I decided to launch my own advertising agency. This was virtually the only way I could spend time with my (at the time) small son, because I became a mom and dad at such a young age that I never stopped living my life. I didn't have a reason to do it. To the contrary! I now had the greatest motivation of all to succeed. From day one, Juan Sebastian became my life's engine and with my family's full support, I was able to graduate from a career that had always been my passion—and it still is today.

The magic of my profession comes from its essence: it's all about people. People are the target of all marketing ideas and advertising actions. It is about creativity at its best. Each of us working in this field has a vast array of possibilities in terms of specialization: some prefer photography, others design, while others choose numbers and analysis, new media, traditional media, consumer psychology, etc. The list is endless. I turned to words; I'm good with them, and they are good for everything if you know how to spice them up with a bit of ingenuity.

After reaching many goals and putting aside many others over time; after living in a world of experiences trickled with success and failures alike—which are never really failures, I prefer to call them "lessons learned"—and after undertaking risks and meeting challenges so demanding that only I could have imagined them, the only thing I wanted at thirty-two (that's how old I was when I came to America) was to live a quiet life. And, though it may seem paradoxical, in Miami—a very lively city by night and day—it's possible to achieve just that.

You can live the life you chose to live anywhere, regardless of circumstances; and I have managed to create my own universe here. I work doing what I like—writing—and to the extent possible, I spend as much leisure time as I can with my loved ones.

...Writing, yes! And precisely—reading and writing—were turning into a challenge; a challenge that was almost impossible to meet! There was just one thought in my head: that not only the nature of my "quiet life" was crumbling, but my life itself was about to change.

I left the office that Monday and was on my way to the doctor's office determined to resolve the matter of my ophthalmologist appointment; I decided not to announce my visit with a phone call to avoid further excuses.

A few weeks prior, lights had started to bother me, but when I left the building that day, it was more intense. I felt the sunlight on my eyes as if it were a mighty spotlight shining on me. I temporarily solved the problem by wearing sunglasses.

As I was driving...*—Oh my God! Now what?!—*The tall buildings far off in the horizon were void of windows and doors; the shapes had begun to lose sharpness. I knew that there were buildings in the background, because I could see an outline, but I was unable to distinguish any details. "I don't want to think about it… I don't want to think at all!!! I need to stay calm, if I get stressed out it will be worse, by now I know this is progressively deteriorating and I am going to find a solution. *Everything is going to be fine.*"

The road

Upon arriving at the office, of course the appointment for the ophthalmologist was non-existent, and I was not willing to accept another excuse. I just could not! I was on a race against time.

"Paola, don't worry. We're going to get your appointment today and we will call you with the information."

"So, with whom is the appointment you're trying to get?" I asked them, this time without a smile and firmly.

From the back of an office, I could hear a lady somewhat irritated saying, "If you can't wait, why don't you get the appointment yourself?"

When I heard that—totally disregarding the rude comment—I felt like a bucket of cold water was poured over me, realizing *my lack of knowledge* about what I thought was the "protocol." I replied in awe, "Can I get the appointment myself?" To which the receptionist said, "Yes, of course. Since we are familiar with the procedure, we try to get appointments with the *(…) Institute* (he says the name and I see it written on a paper, but I rather not disclose it, for obvious reasons, I have also decided not to disclose the name of this doctor and his staff)."

Ha!... I shake my head in disagreement "No! Give me the Doctor's referral and I'll make the appointment myself." They did exactly that and I left.

Thanks to the insensibility of these people I had lost precious time… but there was no point on crying over spilled milk, meeting with an Ophthalmologist was now in my own hands.

"…But, which one should I choose?" It was clear that it had to be a very good one. I had no time for improvisation or lack of experience. The problem was, I didn't know any. "What should I do, now?"

When I got home, Sebastian saw my distress; without giving him details of the degree of my problems and symptoms, or motives for my urgency, I told him what had happened with the appointment I never received. He listened attentively and then asked a question—though he knew the answer already—a question that would completely obliterate my up to then "discreet silence" about the whole thing.

"Did you speak to David about this?"

"No! He has enough things to worry about already, I don't want to bother him by adding one more."

"You need to talk to him! He will tell you what to do, I'm positive. Plus, you know he *must* know a good ophthalmologist."

…After a few seconds in silence, accepting that he was absolutely right, I replied that I was in fact going to speak to David. It was exactly what I did that very night (without going into the details about why I needed to see a good ophthalmologist so urgently).

Without a second thought, David gave me the contact of one of the top specialists at *Bascom Palmer Eye Institute*.

David is one of the best human beings I have ever met. Honest, with solid values, principles and sublime attributes—it was impossible for me not to fall in love hopelessly, reciprocating all the love, care, respect, and protection with which he "embraced my life" from the beginning.

I met David little after arriving in America, and from that time on, we were not able to part from each other. It was only a few years later—due to inevitable professional circumstances—that thousands of miles of distance settled between us. Still, the mutual profound emotional connection, support, and sense of protection never vanished.

Nothing happens in vain, and I always knew that, in addition all the endlessly wonderful moments we lived in a relationship bonded by an "indescribably special" connection, I had met David for an extraordinary reason, and the answer was beginning to manifest itself.

With a clear path to follow—a path that I fully trusted, laid out and sustained by him–, I called *Bascom Palmer* very early in the following morning, trying to get an appointment with the specialist suggested by David, but when I explained my case to the person at the other end of the line, she told me that I need something else, that I did not have to worry, they were going to refer me to the right person. She started asking routine questions to start the registration process and set up the appointment.

Unfortunately, the *Bascom Palmer Eye Institute* was not within the network of my health insurance provider, so I had to get an authorization from them. I immediately interpreted this as "more time," my other option was a *Plan B* (the shorter road), which was obtaining the appointment privately; in this case, numbers started to play a very important role to account for my budget.

Bascom Palmer Eye Institute is recognized worldwide as one of the top and most advanced centers dedicated to ophthalmological care, research and education. It has a professional team of specialists who are globally recognized, and it is the No. 1 ophthalmological hospital in the United

States of America, certified by the American Board of Ophthalmology.

...In other words, David could not have given me a better recommendation. We were sure we would find a solution to my problem there—with or without insurance coverage. I had to get the appointment and it had to be now. So, I decided to go for *Plan B* (private financing), but before, I had to exhaust every last resource of *Plan A*.

I got on the ball to get the authorization from my insurance, but what I did not know was that the authorization had to be requested by my PCP—the one who was unable to get me the appointment! And, although throughout the two days that followed I tried to get the authorization from them, it was—not surprisingly—"impossible." Thus, I had to move on to *Plan B*.

They say the last thing you may lose is faith, and as my problem progressed, my faith became more and more substantial, pressing down the other side of the scale, becoming also more profound.

Those last few nights had become an incessant, silent plea asking for my eyes to return to normal the following morning. I tried keeping them shut as much as possible, foolishly thinking that resting them would restore my eyesight. But, to the contrary, my symptoms were becoming increasingly evident.

When I woke up that Thursday, I felt a constant discomfort on my left eye... a relentless dryness and dull pain. I was emotionally declining, which was even worse; and I was avoiding to cry, because my sight was already blurry enough to add to it tears and congestion.

"Baby, do you already have an appointment at *Bascom Palmer*?" asked David, very mindful of my agility to solve my issue, even when he knew very little of the actual symptoms I was having. I did not want him to be overly concerned.

"I have been trying to get an authorization from my insurance," I explained.

"Forget the insurance! Get the appointment as soon as possible. You know that you can fully rely on my support and what's important now is your appointment."

I could perceive his worry in the tone of his voice and that's exactly what I was trying to avoid. I hate to be the cause of anxiety in those whom I love, that's why I was not disclosing any details about the whole thing up to now; but on the other hand, it is those who love us most the ones who can give us the greatest strength and motivation, who inspire us to go on in spite of circumstances. His words became a haven in the midst of chaos— he has an extraordinary gift to make one feel as if everything is under control.

I took my cellphone and called *Bascom Palmer* again, this time requesting a private appointment, which was set up with a Doctor Dumbar, for the following Monday, April 25th. This became my new beacon of hope and optimism.

Week 8 – Not a damn thing!

—...And the guy thought I was flirting with him—

That Monday, having lunch at the food plaza near the office, I said hello to a man who was coming in my direction, at about twenty steps from me. I waved, because, even though I could not see him clearly, I was convinced it was Nick. He lifted his hand and as he was waving back, getting closer to me (now three steps away, not twenty), I realized he was a total stranger. "I'm sorry, I thought you were someone else" I said, as he brushed past me and into the restaurant. Laughing, I thought to myself—the last thing I needed: I can't even recognize people!

No matter how meaningful our own problems are, or how immense the "positive" or "negative" impact of an event in our lives, the truth is, the world keeps on spinning, the show must go on, and so must we.

Long gone were those days in which I could focus on a specific subject and isolate it from everything, as if nothing else existed. The list of things I had to pay attention to was long, and distractors—or as I call them, energy thieves—had to remain inconsequential.

It was clear that I was confronting a new reality for which I was not prepared. In fact, I did not even know what my reality was, but it was mine, along with my worries, and nobody, absolutely nobody—

by my own choice—really knew the severity of the issues, since I kept concealing it, as discreetly as possible, until I found out what exactly was wrong.

The workload at the office did not stop, in fact, it grew every day, and every day it became more difficult for me to meet the demand. I had to buy time without arousing suspicion. After all, there was only one week left before chaos would unravel.

In those last few weeks, I practically abandoned my desk and moved into the second floor living room in the office, where I had some more privacy and the only ones who would sit with me once in a while were Nick and Jen—an ideal situation.

"Pao, how is the issue of your eyes? Are you still having difficulty seeing well with the new glasses you got?" Jen asked me ever so delicately, as she saw me with my head pressed against the PC monitor, moving it up and down and side to side, trying to read whether what I wrote was correct.

With a shy smile, trying to make fun of the situation and putting my best face forward I replied, "Well, I can't see a damn thing! But I already have an appointment at the *Bascom Palmer Eye Institute* for next Monday." *"Bascom Palmer?"* she asked, somewhat surprised. "You go to *Bascom Palmer* when there's something really wrong with your eyes" she concluded. I briefly shared with her some of my symptoms; when I told her I cannot see clearly up close or far away, that I cannot see whether a building has windows or doors, but only the outline, and that the same goes for people who are right next to me "I know you're there and it's you, because I know you, but don't tell me to describe your features because I cannot see your face distinctly". In apprehension, she said "yes... that's not normal! That's a good reason to go to *Bascom Palmer*... But don't worry, you're going to be fine. They will help you. When it comes to the eyes, they're the best."

Sparkles

It's Friday, and I get up from bed full of enthusiasm, and why not, happiness! Perhaps because I know that this will be the last day of sacrifice at the office. I was going to rest during the weekend, I wasn't planning on getting out of the house; come Monday, my eyesight woes would become a thing of the past and everything would get back to normal. Yes: I was happy!

I get into the bathroom to get ready. I can't see myself in the mirror—Who cares! It's nothing new.– Although every morning I was awaiting with great anticipation that my symptoms would disappear, or at least that one of them would subside, they remained with me, and—surprise, surprise!—one more was joining the list. Ironically, this one was beautiful. A clear, pure white burst of light; a sparkle I saw through my right eye and made me think of a small but radiant star. Truth be told, although it seemed beautiful, given my circumstances I should have thought of a "short circuit"; it sounds funny, but I could not allow myself to think of it as a positive thing, I knew that I had to pay attention to this new symptom, and of course, mention it in detail to the ophthalmologist, along with all the other symptoms.

There were three flashes in total: the first in my right eye and the other two in my left eye. They all occurred at different times, between that day and the day of my appointment.

"Mike, I'm going to see the ophthalmologist on Monday at 10:30 am. As soon as I'm done there, I'll come to the office."

"Sure, no worries. Let me know how it goes."

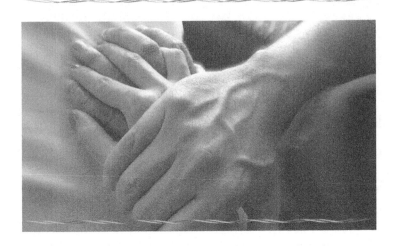

Week 9 – The dance

April 25th, 2016.

The day of my appointment arrived. How exciting! I woke up a bit earlier than usual. I was anxious, optimistic, holding on to the thought that everything would be solved. I remember precisely what I was wearing that day. No high heels. I wanted to wear something comfortable, but smart enough to be able to go to the office after *Bascom Palmer*'s, so I opted for dark blue jeans, a red silk blouse with short sleeves and blue flats with red lace trimming and bow, matching my top.

"Ma, do you want me to go with you?"

"No love, don't worry. I don't know how long it's going to take me and I have to go to work afterwards. I'll call you and let you know how it goes as soon as I find out."

For breakfast, I make myself an oatmeal (a light breakfast) and while I'm eating, I carefully think through everything I must tell the ophthalmologist. I could not forget any detail. I finish and take my purse, the folder documenting the tests and results up to then and my car keys… "Wait a minute, I think I better not drive!" That was my first thought when I held the car keys in my hand. I was in no condition to drive, it was a risk for me and others. Instead, I took an Uber.

When I arrived at *Bascom Palmer Eye Institute*, I went to the information booth and was told to go through hall A. "Where's the 'A'?" I asked, pointing with my finger trying to guess where it was. The young woman looked at me and realized I was not able to see what she was pointing at—which I later discovered was an *enormous* letter A—so, she walked me over to my designated area. I only waited a few minutes before someone called my name. I was lead into a cubicle where Orquidea Ruiz, a woman with a friendly smile and warm voice welcomed me and started to ask me some basic questions to register my appointment and initiate the check-in.

As I began telling her in much detail why I was there, I gave her the folder I had brought with me to reference the previous exams. She examined it carefully and after a few minutes, as she read them, she said: "but, why did they give you an appointment with Doctor Dumbar? He is excellent, but he is an optometrist, and you've already been seen by two optometrists. You need to see an ophthalmologist." She looked behind her, read a paper next to her and told me that there were no available appointments with any of the ophthalmologists on duty that day. She got up from her chair, hugging my folder and spoke: "give me a moment," and she left the room.

I remember closing my eyes and thinking: *For heaven's sake!* I could not grasp the fact that I did not have an appointment with the right doctor... I waited patiently.

A few minutes went by before she returned, somewhat apologetic for the wait, but in good spirits: "Paola, I am sorry for the wait, but the good news is I was able to get you an appointment for today with one of the ophthalmologists in the house. I spoke to Doctor... (she told me, but I can't remember his name) and he was going to agree to see you, but he just got called for an emergency and had to cancel all his appointments for today, he had to hurry over to the *Jackson Memorial Hospital.* So, I went to speak to another specialist and he will see you. His name is Dr. Eric Hansen, he is a remarkable expert. I took the liberty of showing him your folder with the exams and explained to him about all the money you've already spent and the time you've invested so far to no avail. Without a second thought, he accepted your case and he will see you shortly." I just looked at her and sighed, smiling, as I uttered a big "THANK YOU!" For a moment there I thought I was going to have to go back home and wait for another appointment with a different doctor… I felt I could breathe again.

Orquidea immediately finished setting me up in the system, gave me back my folder and added another folder that I should turn over to Dr. Hansen. Now, I only had to wait to be called into the practice.

I think not even ten minutes went by, when I heard my name. First, they took me into an office for initial questions and assessment, the type of information shared with the ophthalmologist a few minutes prior to the consultation. I distinctly remember that the doctor who received me first and asked me those first questions was very attentive to the symptom of sparks of light and not being able to see very large letters in one of the walls inside that room, as he was testing my eyesight with the typical "Read the first line" (which you have to read from the other side of the room). "What line?" I asked. He turned around, looked towards the wall and looked back at me; I glanced at him and said, "I don't see them, I can't see any letters or numbers... I just can't see it!"

"Calm down, Dr. Hansen will see you now, I will talk to him." He got up, went out of the consultation room leaving my folder and the report on the desk back in the room and shortly thereafter, a different physician came in.

"Paola?"

"Yes"

"I'm Dr. Hansen, nice to meet you."

He shook my hand and sat down.

It's hard to describe the kindness and sense of trust and professionalism that he projected from the very first second of my meeting with Dr.

Hansen. I told him the whole story, without skimming on all the details of my condition.

After completing some exams that I was already quite familiar with, he proceeded to perform additional color-based exams. I remember he asked me to identify specific features from a book and I could only see blotches and images as one whole smudge. He proceeded to take one of several bottles with different-colored caps and asked me what color was each one of them. I went on to do yet another exam, so I guess I probably failed that one. But it did not matter: Dr. Hansen was determined to find the fault in my eyes. He sent me off to undergo two more tests—macula and visual field—which I was able to complete that same day, right there at *Bascom Palmer's*. Although I did not have a previous appointment, for some reason, I was able to complete each test, and I was even seen before other people who had made appointments. For one of the exams, there was no available appointment, but I took the place of a patient that never arrived and was able to return to Dr Hansen's office with both results on that very same day.

We were well into the afternoon and we were still looking for the root of the problem. Doctor Hansen saw the results I brought and told me we needed to do additional tests, two different types of MRIs.

"Ok, can I do those here? Let me know and I'll just get them over with right now."

For starters, I had no clue what an MRI was, and secondly, I was absolutely focused on completing every single test that could get me closer to my goal, which was, if not "not leaving this place until I can see again," at least knowing the cause of the problem to begin correcting it. The one thing that was not in my list of options was to exit in the same condition in which I entered. I was resolved to faithfully abide by every test that the doctor requested—as soon as possible—to help him get to a diagnosis. That's exactly what I was doing. If at that point every prior test was not providing an answer, we had to proceed to the next step with optimism and confidence.

Obviously, easier said than done. In fact, reality was different.

"Paola, MRIs can be done here, but I think you have to obtain coverage from your insurance, because these are very costly exams and we need two of them," he explained, as he filled out the referral to get them done without difficulties. He concluded saying that he was giving me a new appointment in eight days, but if I were to be able to do it before, to "please" let him know by sending him a text message (he wrote down his phone number in one of the documents).

I looked at him, took a deep breath and replied to him that if they could do those tests here at *Bascom Palmer*, I'd rather do it at once... "how costly are they?" I asked him. "I don't know exactly, but certainly thousands of dollars. Go down to radiology and ask them if they have an appointment available."

I obtain the referral from him and go directly to radiology. There, I meet Andrea Vieira and give her the referral. She reviews her system and tells me the next available appointment is in fifteen days and also gives me the total cost of those two exams.

"Fifteen days! Oh, no!!! Don't you have anything, anything at all before then?" I briefly explain to her the reason for my urgency.

She looks at me and tells me "Give me your phone number, if someone cancels, I'll call you.".

I did not have all that money! Much less all that time! At that moment, my world crumbled to pieces, my sense of helplessness was immense, I knew that in fifteen days, like the extinguishing flame of a candle, the light in my eyes would go off. In other words, fifteen days meant absolute blindness.

Right then and there, I receive a text message from David, asking how my appointment was; I reply sending him a picture of the MRI referral that Dr. Hansen gave me and I tell him that everything is much more serious than I previously thought. He calls me immediately, I take a seat in the waiting room, as far as possible from others. I cannot contain my tears. I was panic-stricken. I tell him that I cannot see, that I *really cannot see much at all*, that I do not have fifteen days.

Upon hearing this and seeing the picture of the MRIs referral—which, as opposed to me, he *was* familiar with and understood—he asks me what is the cost of the exams. At that very second— miracles do exist—that very second, without knowing anything about my phone call, Andrea asks me to get closer to the counter (I do it with David on the line), and at the same time, as if they were timing it, David tells me that the money is already in my account, while Andrea asks me whether I can do the MRI right now, that she's going to squeeze me in before the next patient.

Almost without understanding what had just happened, letting myself be guided like a passenger in a rollercoaster ride—and after feeling such emptiness—I regain hope. I calm down, and since I cannot see very well, Andrea helps me fill out a form that I must complete before taking the exam. Right after doing so, I go into a room with a massive device. As soon as I see it, I finally understand and reckon what an MRI is.

Almost two hours later, immediately upon finishing, I write a text message to Doctor Hansen:

"Doctor Hansen, I have the MRI results with me, I was able to do them right here at *Bascom Palmer*, are you still here?"

I look at the watch, evening is falling, the doctor isn't replying, so I go up to his office. The whole floor is practically empty. Only two people at the information booth. I turn around and there is

Doctor Hansen, talking on his cellphone. He looks at me and makes a signal with his hand, letting me know he will be with me in a minute.

He hangs up, calls me over and asks me to follow him into his office, as I excitedly tell him how I managed to get the MRIs done right there. I show him the CD Andrea gave me, although she told me he would be able to see the results in the system.

He says "yes", confirming he has indeed seen the result already. He kindly asks me to sit down and takes a seat across me, thanking me for my agility in completing every exam he asked throughout the day and confirms he knows the root of the problem.

"I can't believe it! We did it… We did it!" I think enthusiastically.

"What is it? What's the problem?! What is the next step? Do I need glasses?"

He turns to look at his monitor, then looks back at me; moves his chair closer to mine and asks:

"Paola, do you have any family here with you?"

"Yes. My son, but he is home." Naively, I assumed the doctor thought I had come with my car and for obvious reasons, besides the fact that they dilated my pupils, I was unable to drive back home, so someone else should drive me.

"How old is your son?"

"He is 20 years old, but I didn't bring my own car, don't worry, I don't have to drive."

He ignores my answer about the car and just looks at me, he seems pensive. He asks me one more question...

"Besides your son, is another family member here with you?"

"My boyfriend, but he is travelling outside of the country."

He sighs, stopping as if to gain momentum—or take a breath—and tells me in the gentlest tone, if tainted with a veil of anguish:

"OK, Paola, the reason why you've been losing your eyesight and displayed those symptoms is because there's a considerably large tumor in your head. It is pressing against the optic nerves in both eyes—" he began to explain the findings as clearly as possible. It's not easy to find plain words to explain a diagnosis of such consequence, however, he managed to do so, while showing me on his monitor the images of a tumor right in the center of my head. "Is it… all of this!?" I interrupted, pointing (at what I could barely see). "Yes," he replied.

I stared at him as he kept on explaining the situation. I suppose the news affected me in such a way—given the size of the tumor and its location—that his voice began to gradually fade away…

I come back to my senses, let him finish (as I always do), absorbing the essence of the information, I do a classic *Paola*, briefing him back on what he had just told me:

"OK, let's see if I understood clearly: the cause of my problem is that I have a huge tumor in the middle of my head right next to my brain and if I don't have surgery right now I will become completely blind and then, I will die." (I told him that was my interpretation of his professional medical diagnosis, which he had articulated so fittingly and gently, but I was repeating it in my own words and more than words, in my own *style*. At any rate, this was all I needed to understand. How the message was conveyed was the least of our worries now).

"Right"–he replied somewhat reluctantly to my conclusion after a pause.

A deafening silence followed. I could do nothing but stare at him. I felt as if the world stopped spinning. There were no tears, no howling in despair, no fainting... nothing of the sort. I was simply there, composed, motionless, taking in the situation; he stared back, perhaps awaiting a reaction from me. "OK... this is happening and it's happening to me, right here, right now," my mind was telling myself. I was undoubtedly not ready to discover an issue of such a scale and I had no clue what I should do next. I could only manage to turn to the one person that made me feel as if everything was under control, no matter what happened, and who made sure that *everything was going to be alright*. That one person who did not allow absolutely anything bad to happen to me ever since we met: David.

"Can I ask you a favor? Can you please accurately and in every detail explain to my boyfriend with your terminology, not mine, everything you just told me? Then, I'll go straight to Boston and his brother can perform the surgery, he is one of the top oncologists worldwide."

"Sure, I can talk to him, but perhaps you haven't quite understood. You don't have time to fly to Boston. You can't even go back home to get your things. You need to go into surgery right now! Dr. Komotar is waiting for you this minute at *The University of Miami Hospital.*"

While Dr. Hansen talks, I'm calling David; he cannot pick up the phone and sends a message telling me he is on a conference call and will call me back as soon as he finishes. For the first time in the years we've been together I reply telling him: "Love, it's urgent!" Not a second goes by and he is calling back. I let Dr. Hansen pick up the phone.

While they speak, I get up, take a deep breath—I think I took in all the oxygen in the room into my lungs—I close my eyes and with the heaviest heart I sink my head in contemplation: *Dear Lord, is this how it ends? Is this the conclusion of my story?*

And then, I feel a breeze that fills me with peace... a profound sense of tranquility, a serenity I can't explain in words. In a matter of seconds, I understand all the amazing things that happened that day, things that normally don't happen, but they did, and they were perfectly synchronized— like clockwork! At that time I didn't know it, but *more events were still to unfold.* I only knew that everything was going to be fine. I realized that *I was in the midst of a dance of angels and miracles, working together to save my life... each one of them doing their best.*

The gift

I remember I could hear in David's voice he was overwhelmed, but in charge, asking questions and making all the necessary arrangements, ensuring I would obtain everything that I needed and that he could provide from afar. He explained to Dr. Hansen that he was out of the country, and asked him to place me in the best hands and help me manage everything from that point forward. Dr. Hansen assured him that my case being handled by Dr. Komotar, one of the top neurosurgeons in the clinic. After a few additional minutes talking, they hung up, and David sent me a text message that was at once deeply encouraging, loving, and full of optimism. He was giving me instructions, giving me strength, and giving me peace, reassuring me that *everything was going to be fine*. He asked me to please strictly adhere to the doctors' orders… I could feel the warmth of his embrace and the strength of his hand in mine within each word I read, offering all the confidence and solace I needed.

Dr. Hansen explained to me how to get to the emergency department at the University of Miami Hospital, where Dr. Komotar was awaiting me, as he was writing down some notes. He asked me when was the last time I had something to eat, because it was important to refrain from eating before surgery; I told him I had only had oatmeal for breakfast before coming in, and that was at 8:30 a.m. After that I only had a coffee while waiting for the macula exam, around noon. That was all.

"You didn't have lunch?"

"No. I was fully focused on getting all the exams you asked for." He smiled at me. "I'm glad you did."

It is remarkable when I think about everything that happened that day, as if all circumstances were aligned on my favor: I did not bring my car, I did not eat, timing was perfect, there were no obstacles; all conditions, appointments, and budgets granted... Angels and miracles at every turn.

It is almost 7:00 p.m. on that same Monday when I leave Dr. Hansen's office; I now have to face one of the toughest parts: I have to call my son!

I look at my phone, it only has five percent battery. I remember I saw a cellphone charging station in the ophthalmology waiting room. I walk there and connect my cellphone for a few minutes; I sit down and with my head tilted, I try to make out the red bow on my blue shoes that I so like, to no avail. A thought comes to mind —I can't believe it, instead of running over to the emergency department I come here to charge my phone instead! And then, uh-oh! I see Dr. Hansen standing right in front of me...

"Paola, you can't lose any time, you have to go now, the doctors are waiting for you." I look back at him and tell him I must call my son and my family in Colombia and my cellphone is about to die. He understands but asks me not to take longer than ten minutes.

I think he was surprised to see how calm I was, but actually more than being calm, I was trying to save my energy and optimism for what was coming, and I could only do so by remaining at peace and composed, in spite of the circumstances.

The ten minutes were not up when I disconnected my phone and rushed over to the emergency room at University of Miami Hospital.

As per the doctor's indications, it would take me about fifteen minutes to walk from one building to the other, but when I was about to leave the Bascom Palmer building, I had already forgotten the route he had described –everyone who knows me knows that this is pretty normal. My sense of orientation is unreal, it just doesn't exist. So, at the exit, I asked the security guard how to get there...

"You have to go there now?"

"Yes, I have to be admitted."

Without further questions, he looked at me, briefly smiled and told me "Don't worry, I'll ask one of my coworkers to take you." And so he did.

On the way, I called my son:

"Hi, ma."

"Loki!" (one of the many affectionate nicknames I have for him) I say hello in my usual tone.

"How was the appointment? Did you go to work?"

"Sweetie, I need a favor. Write down this address (I dictate it to him), now, take one of those small suitcases I have in my closet and put in it: the black sweatpants, one of the pink *Kiss* t-shirts, the one with the V-neck, the grey blazer, one of my sleeping tops, socks, underwear, the cellphone charger, and toiletries, my toothbrush, toothpaste, deodorant, and so on, and also please bring the same for you, so you can stay here with me."

"OK, but why? What happened?"

"I'm just going to have a minor surgery, they know what I have, but when you get here I will explain, because I almost have no battery left on my phone. I love you. Don't take long."

"OK, ma, I'm on my way."

One of the typical features that defines me as a person is my way of saying things, of sharing news; always direct, transparent, and without embellishments. This time I could not do it, at least not with my son; and to be honest, I think that was part of the reason why I asked Dr. Hansen to answer David's call.

I also had to call my brother in Colombia, and it had to be done before Sebastian's arrival at the hospital. My plan was to tell my son face to face and peacefully what was really happening before being admitted (it was no minor surgery what I was having), at that point, my brother could be Sebastian's support... My poor brother! I almost killed him with the news:

"Hi Chin." (I generally don't use anyone's name, only affectionate nicknames.)

"Hi! How was this morning's appointment? Did you get a new prescription?"

I took in a deep breath... or maybe it was to gain momentum, enough momentum to launch a jumbo. I had to disclose the whole breadth of the news in just a few words:

"Chin, I'm still here. This is what's going on: I almost have run out of charge on my phone, please promise me you won't tell our parents anything, because I don't want things to get any harder, I don't want them to get a heart attack. Don't tell Piti either, because she will worry. We found the problem. I have a very large tumor right in the middle of my head and it's squeezing the optic nerve and the brain. I have to go into surgery now."

For a few seconds there's absolute silence on the other side…

"Hello?"

"…*OOOK*…" he whispers very slowly.

"I'm here alone, but I'm fine. I have not told Sebastian yet, I'm waiting for him to arrive; I need you to please stay in touch with him. The only people who know what's going on are David and you. David already spoke to the doctor. I am going to tell Sebastian and Mike, from work; I don't want anyone else to know for now. I don't want to trouble them.

After the silence, he sort of snapped back and—as clueless as I was in terms of what to do—asked me:

"So, listen, what should I do?"

"Never you mind, you don't need to do anything, don't even think about coming here. I'm in the best of hands and doing exactly what I have to do. Now, when Sebastian gets here, I will charge my phone and I'll call you back."

"...*OK*. I'm going to stay in touch with him. He will need some support when you are admitted, because he will be alone. So... Paola, can I at least tell Martica?"

My heart grew warm with his question; I found it funny and replied: "Of course! Martica is your wife, for me you are both one and the same person. I will call you later. Don't worry. Everything is going to be fine!"

As I hung up, Sebastian arrived (calm as ever), suitcase strapped around his shoulder. He kissed me on the cheek; I looked at him and smiled, got the charger out of my bag and asked one of the people at the emergency patients' check-in desk to let me charge my cellphone.

Brain tumor is the type of diagnose that you never want to see next to your name, much less so when you're thirty-six years old and you have a long list of amazing things you still want to do, have to do!—before that inevitable appointment arrives, the one you assume will be waiting for you many years ahead.

Still, I learned that the worst in these situations is not your own pain, but the sorrow and agony that you can unintentionally inflict on your dearest ones, on those whom love you and you love back. They suffer more than you when they see you hurt or in danger, you don't want to lose them, and they don't want to lose you.

How could I explain to my son that his mother was walking a very fine line and everything could radically change from that day forward? Now it wasn't just about losing my eyesight. What up to a few minutes was my greatest fear came to be, perhaps, the least of my worries, maybe that was the "least worst" that could happen to me.

"Loki, come here, let's go outside for a minute while we wait for them to call me in."

We stood just outside of the emergency room, towards the right, just past the door, so we wouldn't block people and avoid distractions. I began explaining to him what was happening with great subtlety but realistically; he took it the same way.

I think we accepted it so, because we were ignorant about the matter, none of us was able to grasp the scale of the situation, its relevance, and the medical risks. That's why we stayed calm and put all our faith and hope in the hands of the doctors. We were already doing what we should, what was in our power to do. Although everything was happening to me, I felt it was my duty to project a sense of serenity in the presence of my son—I think, at that moment, I managed to do so.

Suddenly, a hospital attendant came to get me.

"Paola Garcia?"

"Yes. It's me and this is my son."

"You need to sign some intake forms. Please, come with me."

I follow, sign the documents, they tell me everything is ready, I just need to wait a couple of minutes. I go get my cellphone, I still had one more important call to make. I had to call my office and tell them what was happening. I call Mike, he is unable to pick up the phone so I write him a message telling him that I'm going into surgery and I might not be able to work the next few days. A few minutes later, he calls me back, I quickly let him know everything and tell him I'm worried and I don't want to lose my job. His voice changes, he is no longer my boss, but a friend.

"Paola, don't you worry about a thing, forget your job, at this time that's the least of your worries, you're not going to lose it. Moreover, if you want, I can keep this confidential and only discuss it with people who need to know: the CEO and the head of Human Resources, no one else."

"Thank you, Mike."

"I will take care of everything over here, there's nothing to worry about, you're in a good hospital. Please ask Sebastian to keep me updated."

At that point, like an ominous cloud settling in, it dawned on me that I might never again go back to work; I started contemplating my two options…

"Mike…"

"Yes."

"I am afraid… very afraid."

"No, don't you worry. Everything is going to be fine!"

I breathe in deeply, close my eyes and drop my head in reflection…

"Yes… yes, you're right, *everything is going to be fine*. Thank you for everything. I will keep you on the loop, I will give Sebastian your number. Bye."

"Bye. And do not worry."

After speaking to Mike, I sat down next to Sebastian, I looked at him and realized I was facing yet another moment of truth: what will happen if I can't go back home with him?

If that was going to be the end, I had to try to leave everything as organized as possible, before it would become chaotic. I called my brother again to give him a list of things that I had pending one way or another, to make my son's future life easier, I had to explain how to resolve those pending matters; in other words, I started making a difficult "life inventory," a record of my stuff, *without* me; things that from that moment forward and forever, would change in terms of priority and value. I find myself unable to express with words what I was feeling as I explained to my brother one by one, every element of that inventory. I was speaking about a future of which I was not going to be a part.

I remember that a few years ago someone asked me that cliché question: "If you could turn back time, knowing everything that has happened in your life up to now, up to what point would you go back?" My answer was clear and immediate: "I would go back up to the day that my son was born, because I simply cannot conceive of my life without him in it."

There are people who say that God's plans are perfect. I'm one of them. I learned not to question those plans; instead, I learned to have faith in them.

My son was born when I was fifteen years old. From that point forth, I understood that life had not simply given me "a child," it gave me much more than that; it gave me enormous wings in the shape of a little boy, wings that would grow along with him. It gave me the strength, the will to go on in spite of the circumstances. It gave me motivation, joy, warmth, the most unconditional and pure love of all. It has been Sebastian who, by merely existing, has pushed me far beyond my limits; he has made me set almost unreachable goals, and then—for him— I have reached them! He is the one who makes me ponder on whether to make one decision over another, and whether that decision will set an example for him. It is because of him that I feel proud every day, and every day I feel the need of being a better person, because he deserves it.

Yes, life gave me the most precious gift of all, and what was happening to me at that time was no compelling reason to give up or lose my faith. On the other side of the scale I had much more valuable reasons to go on, with all my positivism and energy.

Matrix

Here we go, no extra time, no extensions, it's showtime! It's time to put my faith to the test, time for trusting.

I was admitted and while everyone at the hospital saw preparations for brain surgery(!), I saw what looked like me getting ready to audition for a new *Matrix* movie. They started connecting cables here and there, virtually every single activity in my body was registered through different devices.

The best part was the seven cylinder-shaped discs they stuck to my face, around my eyes and forehead. They had been circled in with a black marker, and I was told these were going to be guiding Doctor Komotar during the surgery... —I did not even want to think about what kind of guidance they offered. From that time on, all I did was play around and crack a few jokes with the nurses and doctors about my situation; they laughed and kept saying they could not believe that I was acting like that at that time, but they enjoyed my attitude and it also allowed them to relax and treat me as though they knew me, like family; they treated me with love.

Ultimately, a bad or unwilling attitude on my part was not going to do me any good at all. On the contrary (*remember my theory?*); such attitudes only end up attracting ill-will from people in any situation, and for this one in particular, I assure you, you want to have those huge nurses—some of them almost six feet tall—or even those people who have the "power of a needle" in their hands to treat you with the utmost care and tact. That's how they treated me, all of them, without exception, from the very first moment. Even people who moved me in the stretcher throughout the hospital to get another MRI and other exams needed pre-surgery were being extra careful not to hit the stretcher with the elevator or doors, they went slower when going over a bump, etc. My private room was beautiful and large, it was in a high floor and had a great view of the city, plus an extra bed for visitors, which they set up for Sebastian, right next to mine. Yes, all of them took care of every detail to ensure this experience would be the least traumatic and harsh possible.

When they had to puncture me—no matter how careful the nurse was—a needle is a needle!—it didn't matter how much it hurt, I did not complain.

I might have let out an "ouch!" as I opened my eyes wide and pressed my lips together with my tongue in between, doctors and nurses replying with a smile and a "Sorry!," to which I would answer: "Don't worry, it didn't hurt!" Sebastian would laugh, he knew that it did hurt, a lot!

Somehow we managed to turn the experience into a game. I was taking *selfies* to send to David, who was sad and concerned for me; I sent them to calm him down, and they worked. If he, Sebastian, and my brother would see how strong I was, it would lighten their burden.

Every person I interacted with as I was getting ready for surgery—without exception—spoke marvelously of Dr. Komotar. I remember one of them even emphasized how lucky I was to have him do my surgery. I was anxious to meet him. One of the few things I really wanted to be fully conscious of at the time was that my life was in his hands, so, I definitively wanted to meet him! Every time someone from the hospital came into my room to see me for one reason or another (and there were plenty of reasons, believe me!), I anticipated seeing a doctor with almond-shaped eyes, I tried to imagine how he looked, what was his personality like, his energy...

In their hands

Although the room door was unlocked, there was a *knock knock!*, at the same time that it opened—I wish I could find the right words to describe the amazing and sublime feeling that enveloped me when I saw Dr. Komotar walk in. I immediately knew it was him, even before he introduced himself. He didn't come alone, he came with a colleague: Dr. Sargi would be his partner for my intervention. As I lay just looking at them carefully, I felt how the slight sensation of fear that laid concealed in me began to disappear, until it vanished altogether.

Dr. Komotar sat at the end of the bed, slightly hunched over, hands resting on his knees. Dr. Sargi was standing in front of us and, after he introduced himself, he began explaining every detail of the surgery procedure, its risks, and the role of the devices that were to be used, and their own specific role. Clearly, it was a "delicate" surgery, where that term does not even come close to the degree of risks related to the procedure. One of the MRIs showed that the tumor was not only pressing against the optic nerve, but it opened up around the frontal lobe of the brain, cerebral arteries, etc. The goal was to extract the tumor completely without causing any damage around it. The list of associated risks was long.

What were their roles in the intervention?

Briefly, and in "my own words:" Dr. Sargi was in charge of opening and clearing up the path so that Dr. Komotar could extract the tumor "without causing any damage around it." Afterwards, Dr. Sargi would ensure everything was back on its place. They were the perfect duo! And that was all I needed to know.

While Dr. Sargi talked to me, Dr. Komotar looked at me intently, very calm, and this is what I felt: peace, serenity, and sincere trust.

They wanted to ensure I was aware of the type of surgery and the risks involved. I looked at them, smiled and told them that what I had before my eyes was not only two doctors, but two big angels that I knew were going to give me back my life and that all my faith was in their hands, and in their knowledge.

They smiled and told me to remain calm, reassuring me that *everything was going to be fine...*

"Do you have any questions?"

"Hmm yes, just one. How are you going to get to the tumor?!?" I asked them, as I am drawing an imaginary line in my forehead, side of my head, all the way around it. I was getting used to the idea that I was going to end up with a scar, but I just didn't know where.

"You have nothing to worry about," Dr. Sargi replied, "that's why I'm doing the surgery with Dr. Komotar. I am not going to touch anything aesthetically, everything will be done through the nose."

I opened up my eyes in awe, I think mostly out of happiness, thinking: not touching anything aesthetically?! Wow! I ignored the part about "everything will be done through the nose." For some reason I was keeping at bay any thoughts that might affect my state of peace which I was bent on preserving, I needed all my energy for the surgery. Ultimately, everything else was out of my control. I did not object to anything, I did not question anything, I just allowed them to do their job, fully trusting each one of them. They knew exactly what they were doing.

My case was one with plenty of specifics to keep in mind before taking the right steps, and they did not miss any.

I think every human being needs to hold on to something, a higher force, something that sustains us, gives us faith, hope, a sense of protection. Depending on individual values and beliefs, that something has a name; I call it God, and I speak to Him with trust and respect. He listens to me! He always listens to me.

After almost eighteen intense hours since I had left my house that morning, there was finally some semblance of quietude. Sebastian fell asleep exhausted in the bed visitors bed. Although I was tired and wanted to fall asleep, my thoughts wouldn't let me. I was afraid: infinitely afraid of leaving my son alone, infinitely afraid of not being able to embrace David again, infinitely afraid of not seeing my family ever again. I closed my eyes, and with a heart heavy with humility I only asked God for a little more time, "just a little more time!"

Everything is ready for the surgery to begin; minutes before putting me to sleep, one of the specialists from Dr. Komotar's team performs one last test, he asks me to tell him what letter do I see, showing me his cellphone screen. I don't see any letters, I can barely see his cellphone.

The anesthesiologist's job begins, I fall into a deep slumber...

Intact

Write a book.

After eleven hours under surgery, a "clear" whisper of those words in my ears brings me back to full awareness in the intensive care unit. I open my eyes… "I'm alive!" I think excited. Just then, the specialist who tested me before succumbing to anesthesia comes in. "Hey! Welcome back!" He takes out his cellphone. "What do you see here?" I could see EVERYTHING! I read it all back to him, even the smallest letters. It was a moment of tremendous joy, a shot of pure energy. The doctor seemed surprised and excited, as well. "Wow… It's amazing!" he exclaimed, a huge smile on his face. He was hoping I could see something, but was not expecting I could see everything, even the smallest details. He asked me how I felt overall and left the room.

I spent five days at the clinic, half of them at the intensive care unit, before they gave me the discharge and allowed me to continue recovering at home.

Thanks to an extremely advanced procedure in terms of medical science and technology, together with experience, professionalism, precision, attention to detail, and the true dedication of every single doctor, the surgery was a total success. It was an intervention where the optic nerve, tissue, and cerebral arteries remained intact, I did not present any hormonal unbalance or damage, or any of those things that only doctors know.

The tumor was extracted in its entirety. It was benign. Dr. Komotar and Dr. Sargi, prominent figures in their field, were able to bring me back from this journey absolutely "intact"; my nose was not even swollen, they did not make any incisions nor left external marks, and the period of recuperation and bone regeneration elapsed without incidents. I did not have to take any medications, no antibiotics, not even pain killers or sleeping pills; the recovery could not have been better or faster.

After the surgery, I finally shared the experience with the rest of my family and friends. They were shaken by the news, but at the same time amazed and grateful for the results. I was content with myself for having protected them from extreme distress, informing them only about the problem when it no longer existed.

One year after the intervention all monitoring and tests demonstrate there is no trace whatsoever of the tumor; absolutely nothing in my body was unbalanced or changed. No physical alterations at all and I recovered my eyesight fully: I was "neurologically intact (…)," as per the report of this remarkable experience captured on my medical file.

I had no clue about it, but for years, life had prepared me in a thousand ways for this day. It prepared me in terms of maturity, strength, self-confidence, character, knowledge, hope, decision, humility, and in many other ways. Each event, each factor, each individual who had crossed my path carved the way to get to this precise point, to this precise moment. There are no questions left unanswered; the explanation comes sooner or later.

People say that faith can move mountains. In this case, faith did much more than that. I have no words to describe the immense gratitude I feel for my life every day. And the only explanation I find when I scrutinize the events that unfolded—and how they unfolded—is that it was a mix of science, professionalism, faith, and divine intervention in each and every step of the way. Hence, I could not forget or ignore the three words that woke me up at intensive care. I don't question them and I don't try to find an explanation for them. I simply believed and acted on them, as part of my infinite gratitude.

Every one of us is a unique and incomparable work of art, and so are our lives, diverse in their own individual way. Every single life has its own magic, its own trials and tribulations, its own prizes and rewards; and our attitude in life, along with our decisions, greatly defines the path it takes, the essence of that life.

My grandfather used to say life is not how you want it to be, but how it is, and he was right. But regardless of its hue, life is wonderful, and our profound ability to feel and hold on to it reveals how incredibly alive we are.

We learn more than we think from these experiences. We prove that true love—pure and unconditional—exists and allows you experience life at its fullest; it does not matter how close or far you are from people who love you and whom you love. The effect of love remains the same.

You realize that life can change or cease to exist in the blink of an eye, and though you're no stranger to its ambitions and follies, you also learn that it gives you many wonderful things that you overlooked or did not even take notice of.

The value of everything radically changes; you discover that the simplest of things—such as seeing color or light with absolute clarity—is much more valuable than many material objects you might own or desire.

It is then that you're left with a longing for the embrace of life itself. And nobody can embrace you with life's passion. Nobody can. Life envelopes you like a breeze blowing on your face, a fragrance, the caress of the sea soaking your feet.

You discover that there's nothing that can help you more or make you happier than helping other people.

You enter a spiritual level that was previously unknown to you. Despite all the noise surrounding you, peace and harmony settle into your life, presiding above everything else.

You learn to really *recognize* yourself and more than *knowing* what's good or bad for you, you learn to respect and *enforce* that respect for those things.

Words such as fear, inhibition, and urge, lose their meaning and at the same time, you learn to clearly see and understand the true value of life and its purpose, the meaning of your life.

Remember that nature is wise and your body is a perfect machine. Never ever ignore the signals that your body is sending you, those warning signs letting you know that something inside you is not OK. Pay attention to them and take the right course of action, doing so in due time is critical for the final result..

And, one last piece of advice—for some it might be repetitive and boring, but it is absolutely necessary: please, exercise!

If you're not one already, I'm not asking you to become a professional athlete and win medals, but merely to include a little bit of physical activity in your daily routine, run, walk, take the bike for a spin, go up a flight of stairs, swim, go to the gym, do yoga... choose an endeavor that is also fun for you. There's no better medicine than exercise for healing, prevention, and making you feel better.

It has been a tremendous privilege to be able to write for you. Thank you for taking the time to get to know me, my story, and letting me into your heart.

With love,

Paola

Biographies

- Andrea Vieira
Special tribute to Emily
- Orquidea Ruiz
- Dr. Eric D. Hansen
- Dr. Ricardo J. Komotar
- Dr. Zoukaa B. Sargi
- The author

Andrea Vieira - May 12th, 2016

Andrea Vieira

A native of Río de Janeiro, Brazil, Andrea has lived in the U.S. for over twenty-six years; working in public relations for more than two decades. She is part of *The University of Miami*'s family, having joined it in 2010 as *Hurricane Mom* until 2014, during the time her son Bryan attended this prestigious university. Today, Andrea continues to be an active member of the family, feeling deeply blessed to be part of a team of dedicated individuals who work hard every day to improve and transform the lives of their patients.

Special tribute to Emily

A couple of weeks after my surgery I had to go back for a series of monitoring appointments with each doctor to ensure my body was functioning without any new developments.

After I was done, I went to the radiology department to find Andrea. I wanted to give her a big hug and let her know my deepest gratitude, because if it weren't for "that precise MRI" that I was able to undergo that day—thanks to her and

David (the MRI that showed the tumor and the immediate need of surgery)—I don't even want to think about what could have happened. My story would have been another, with a very different ending.

I hugged her, we cried, and she told me how happy she was, from the bottom of her heart, that everything worked out good for me. She told me she was devoted to her work of helping people, and she dedicated every day to her baby girl Emily, who was also diagnosed with a brain tumor when she was five months old. After intense dedication, devotion, love, and the best care, Andrea told me that her daughter didn't make it.

After listening to her, I could perceive a veil of sorrow dimming her face and I then understood the intensity behind her embrace... I was speechless. Despite a devastating loss such as the one Andrea suffered, she worked day after day honoring her baby girl—a baby girl who, without knowing me, also became my own angel of life.

Thank you, Emily!

Orquidea Ruiz - May 12th, 2016

Orquidea Ruiz

To date, Orquidea Ruiz has worked at *Bascom Palmer Eye Institute* for 11 years, entirely committed to her career; treating each and every patient she encounters with the utmost respect, competence, and kindness.

Thanks to the unconditional love and support of her family—her husband, her son, her parents, and especially her own conviction of wanting to go the extra mile for every single patient—Orquidea recently obtained her A.D.N. and is on her way to obtaining a B.S.N. from the *Miami Regional University.*

Dr. Eric D. Hansen - May 12th, 2016

Dr. Eric D. Hansen, MD

Dr. Eric Hansen, MD obtained his degree from The University of Oklahoma College of Medicine. He completed his ophthalmology residency at Bascom Palmer Eye Institute, University of Miami, followed by an international fellowship at the

University of Utah Health's John A. Moran Eye Center.

Dr. Hansen treated me during his residency at the *Bascom Palmer Eye Institute*, where he discovered the root of my problem. The steps he took reveal his profound humanity, skill, and commitment to his career.

Dr. Ricardo J. Komotar - February 8th, 2017

Dr. Ricardo J. Komotar,

M.D., FAANS, FACS

Dr. Komotar is Associate Professor of Neurological Surgery at the University of Miami School of Medicine. He graduated summa cum laude with a B.S. in neuroscience from Duke

University, spending a year at Oxford University in England to focus on neuropharmacology. He received his medical degree from The Johns Hopkins University School of Medicine with highest honors and completed his internship and neurosurgical residency at Columbia University Medical Center/The Neurological Institute of New York, followed by a surgical neurooncology fellowship at Memorial Sloan-Kettering Cancer Center to specialize in brain tumors.

As Director of the University of Miami Brain Tumor Initiative, Director of Surgical Neurooncology at the University of Miami, Director of the UM Neurosurgery Residency Program, and Director of the UM Surgical Neurooncology Fellowship Program, Dr. Komotar's main clinical interests are surgical and radiosurgical (Gamma Knife) treatment of primary and metastatic brain tumors, as well as meningiomas and pituitary lesions. Dr. Komotar is an internationally recognized leader in the field of brain tumors and performs nearly 700 procedures for these conditions each year using advanced cutting-edge surgical/radiosurgical techniques, making him one of the highest volume brain tumor surgeons in the world.

His research interests include clinical trial development and translational neurooncologic investigations designed to pioneer new therapies for brain tumors. Author of over 500 peer-reviewed scientific articles, book chapters, and invited editorials, Dr. Komotar has received research funding from the National Institutes of Health as well as other national and regional grants. He has served on the Executive Committee for the Congress of Neurological Surgeons and the Executive Board for the AANS/CNS Joint Section on Tumors. He is Founder and Director of the Annual Neurosurgery Charity Softball Tournament to benefit brain tumor research. He is a member of the Society of Neurooncology and reviewer for both Neurosurgery and the Journal of Neurosurgery. Dr. Komotar is also an Emmy ® nominated physician for his work on the series "Breakthrough Medicine".

Dr. Zoukaa B. Sargi - May 12th, 2016

Dr. Zoukaa B. Sargi,
M.D., MPH

Dr. Sargi is originally from Lebanon. He graduated from Medical School in 2000 at Saint Joseph University and earned a very competitive position for Otolaryngology residency. He completed his residency training at Hotel Dieu de France Hospital / Saint Joseph University in June 2005. Following residency, he came to University of Miami where he completed a first fellowship in Rhinology and Endoscopic Skull Base surgery in 2006 and pursued another two-year fellowship in Head and Neck Cancer ablative and microvascular reconstructive surgery. Dr. Sargi subsequently accepted a full time Assistant Professor position in 2008 and has been working as faculty in the department of Otolaryngology since. He started a Master in Public Health during his fellowship and earned the degree from University of Miami in 2013. He was promoted to Associate Professor in June 2014.

Dr. Sargi is very interested in the education and training of students, residents and fellows. He was the proud recipient of the W J Goodwin teaching award in 2010. He served as Clinical Clerkship director between February 2011 and December 2012. He was named Director of the Residency program research in July 2011 and was assigned to oversee the research activity at the level of the residency and fellowships programs. Dr. Sargi continues in this role and serves as mentor for several students, residents and fellows in their research activities.

Paola Garcia

The author

Paola Garcia - Bogota, Colombia, November 26th, 1979 *and* Miami, FL, USA, April 26th, 2016.

After six years of college, I graduated from the Universidad Politécnico Grancolombiano, first with a Technical and later with a Professional Degree in

Marketing and Advertising, focusing on Corporate Communications and laying the foundation for my professional development in the pursuit of ethics, commitment, and excellence.

Since then, I have worked in the development and growth of brands, products, and companies; offering clients the necessary support and becoming a strategic ally in my areas of expertise.

Author, copywriter, and content-editor for web, social media, books, editorials, and the like for multiple media outlets, including the Forbes network, radio stations, multinational companies, and prominent figures from the entertainment industry in Hollywood, such as Phil Cooke.

In terms of the spiritual, I owe my absolute faith and conviction to God. I respect universal individual beliefs, but do not applaud zealotry. I try to go through life letting generosity and kindness lead the way; learning and unlearning, giving my best. My whole life is based on five guiding principles: love, gratitude, integrity, justice, and truth.

www.paolanet.com

@paogarcianet • spanish.copywriter • @Paola_Garcia79

«It is then that you're left with a longing for the embrace of life itself. And nobody can embrace you with life's passion. Nobody can. Life envelopes you like a breeze blowing on your face, a fragrance, the caress of the sea soaking your feet...»

Your notes...